Duty of care for learning disability workers

Justine Barksby and Lucy Harper

Supporting the level 2 and 3 Diplomas in
Health and Social Care (learning disability pathway)
and the Common Induction Standards

LearningMatters

bild

all about people

Acknowledgements

Photographs from www.crocodilehouse.co.uk and www.careimages.com. Our thanks to James and Marianne, and to Choices Housing, The Ridgeway Partnership and Wolverhampton City Council for their help.

First published in 2011 jointly by Learning Matters Ltd and the British Institute of Learning Disabilities

© 2011 BILD

British Library Cataloguing in Publication Data
A CIP record for this book is available from the British Library

ISBN: 978 0 85725 613 3

This book is also available in the following ebook formats:

Adobe ebook ISBN: 978 0 85725 615 7
EPUB ebook ISBN: 978 0 85725 614 0
Kindle ebook ISBN: 978 0 85725 616 4

Cover design by Pentacor
Text design by Pentacor
Project Management by Deer Park Productions, Tavistock
Typeset by Pantek Arts Ltd, Maidstone
Printed and bound in Great Britain by Ashford Colour Press Ltd, Gosport, Hants

Learning Matters Ltd
20 Cathedral Yard
Exeter
EX1 1HB
Tel: 01392 215560
E-mail: info@learningmatters.co.uk
www.learningmatters.co.uk

BILD
Campion House
Green Street
Kidderminster
Worcestershire
DY10 1JL
Tel: 01562 723010
E-mail: enquiries@bild.org.uk
www.bild.org.uk

Contents

This book covers:

- Common Induction Standards   Standard 5 – Principles for implementing duty of care

- Level 2 and Level 3 diploma units SHC 24 – Introduction to duty of care in health, social care or children's and young people's settings, and SHC 34 – Principles for implementing duty of care in health, social care or children's and young people's settings.

Justine Barksby

Justine has been a qualified learning disability nurse since 1995. Since then she has worked as a staff nurse in a learning disability service, she has been a manager of an NHS learning disability day service and also worked as a clinical nurse specialist in challenging behaviour. She is now a lecturer for the University of Nottingham, teaching student nurses. She has a qualification in higher education and is a practice teacher. Justine feels very passionate about the quality of service provision for people with learning disabilities.

Justine lives just outside Nottingham with her fiancé. In her spare time she likes walking and running and even completed the London Marathon.

Lucy Harper

Lucy Harper has worked as a lecturer for the University of Nottingham for five years and is based at the Mansfield site in Nottinghamshire. Before this she spent ten years as a general nurse caring for surgical patients. Lucy is a qualified practice teacher and regularly teaches students from all fields of nursing including learning disabilities. She has always been active in promoting high-quality health care services which are safe and effective for service users, carers, relatives and staff.

Lucy moved to Mansfield 18 years ago to do her nurse training and is now married with two children. She enjoys being with her family and on the rare occasions when she has time to herself, Lucy likes to read or watch films.

Introduction

Who is this book for?

Duty of Care for Learning Disability Workers is for you if you:

- have a new job working with people with learning disabilities with a support provider or as a personal assistant;
- are a more experienced worker who is studying for a qualification for your own professional development or is seeking more information to improve your practice;
- are a volunteer supporting people with a learning disability;
- are a manager in a service supporting people with a learning disability and you have training or supervisory responsibility for the induction of new workers and the continuous professional development of more experienced staff;
- are a direct payment or personal budget user and are planning the induction or training for your personal assistant.

Links to qualifications and the Common Induction Standards

This book gives you all the information you need to complete both the Common Induction Standard on how duty of care contributes to safe practice, and the units *Introduction to duty of care in health, social care or children's and young people's settings* (SHC 24) and *Principles for implementing duty of care in health, social care or children's and young people's settings* (SHC 34) from the level 2 and level 3 diplomas in health and social care. You may use the learning from this unit:

- to help you complete the Common Induction Standards;
- to work towards a full qualification, e.g. the level 2 or level 3 diploma in health and social care;
- as learning for the unit on duty of care for your professional development.

This unit is one of the mandatory units that everyone doing the full level 2 and level 3 diplomas must study. Although anyone studying for the qualifications will find the book useful, it is particularly helpful for people who support a person with a learning disability. The messages and stories used in this book are from people with a learning disability, family carers and people working with them.

Links to assessment

If you are studying for this unit and want to gain accreditation towards a qualification, first of all you will need to make sure that you are registered with an awarding organisation that offers the qualification. Then you will need to provide a portfolio of evidence for assessment. The person responsible for training within your organisation will advise you about registering with an awarding organisation and give you information about the type of evidence you will need to provide for assessment. You can also get additional information from BILD. For more information about qualifications and assessment, go to the BILD website: www.bild.org.uk/qualifications

How this book is organised

Generally each chapter covers one learning outcome from the qualification unit, and one of the Common Induction Standards. The learning outcomes covered are clearly highlighted at the beginning of each chapter. Each chapter starts with a story from a person with a learning disability or family carer or worker. This introduces the topic and is intended to help you think about the topic from their point of view. Each chapter contains the following.

 Thinking points – to help you reflect on your practice.

Stories – examples of good support from people with learning disabilities and family carers.

 Activities – for you to use to help you to think about your work with people with learning disabilities.

Key points – a summary of the main messages in that chapter.

References and where to go for more information – useful references to help further study.

At the end of the book there is:

> **a glossary** – explaining specialist language in plain English.
>
> **an index** – to help you look up a particular topic easily;

Study skills

Studying for a qualification can be very rewarding. However, it can be daunting if you have not studied for a long time, or are wondering how to fit your studies into an already busy life. The BILD website contains lots of advice to help you to study successfully, including information about effective reading, taking notes, organising your time, using the internet for research. For further information, go to www.bild.org.uk/qualifications

Chapter 1

Understand the meaning of duty of care

Peter has lived in this home for the last twenty years. Like the other people who live here he spent a long time in an old long stay hospital for people with a learning disability. He started smoking in the hospital and he still smokes today at least 30 cigarettes a day.

Although Peter has always smoked and it's not something he started when he came to this residential home the staff here feel responsible for supporting Peter to stay healthy. Lots of people including the GP, the learning disability nurse and my colleagues who have known him for a long time have tried to convince him that it would be good for his health to stop smoking. People have explained the risks of smoking to Peter in lots of accessible ways so he can understand. Even so he has decided to carry on smoking.

I know we have a duty of care towards Peter to keep him safe from harm, but Peter is able to make his own decision too! As a new worker it's difficult to know what my duty of care is towards Peter.

Louise, residential support worker

Amina has recently moved into a small flat and is enjoying her own space and independence. She is keen to get better at cooking and wants to be able to make her own breakfast every day so that her support worker doesn't need to come in and help her with it. Together we have looked in detail at what she wants to learn to do such as using the kettle and the toaster. We have also discussed possible risks both with her parents and my manager. It's lovely to see Amina being more independent and having more control over her life. I feel it is part of my duty of care to promote her independence and choices.

Marie, Amina's key worker

Introduction

You might already have come across the term 'duty of care' and need to understand the term and what it means for you in your role as a learning disability worker. This might have been something your manager has spoken to you about or something you have read in the policies and procedures for your place of work. Duty of care is an important concept in social care and as you can see from the two short stories above it is not always easy to explain. It involves both supporting people to stay healthy and safe and promoting their rights and independence. This chapter will help you to provide better support for people with learning disabilities because it will help you to understand how a duty of care affects the people you support, their family carers, the people you work with, you and your employer.

The following learning outcomes from the Common Induction Standards and the mandatory units of the diplomas in health and social care, on duty of care are covered in this chapter.

Learning outcomes

This chapter will help you to:

- understand the meaning of duty of care;
- know why duty of care is important in your work;
- explain what duty of care means in your own role;
- explain how duty of care contributes to the safeguarding and protection of individuals.

This chapter covers:

Common Induction Standards – Standard 5 – Principles for implementing duty of care: Learning Outcomes 1.1 and 1.2

Level 2 HSC 24 – Introduction to duty of care: Learning Outcomes 1.1 and 1.2

Level 3 HSC 34 – Principles for implementing duty of care: Learning Outcomes 1.1 and 1.2

Understand the meaning of duty of care

There are two elements to the idea of duty of care. The first is a duty to avoid acts or omissions (an omission is when you forget or fail to do something), which may cause harm to others. The second is a duty to promote the rights, independence and choices of the person we support.

1. There is a requirement for all of us in society to take reasonable care to avoid injury to others because of our thoughtless or careless acts or omissions. For example, as a driver we have a duty of care to passengers in our car, pedestrians, cyclists and other road users as well as owners of property by the road. As well as this broad common law duty of care we also have a more specific legal duty of care as a social care employee set out in a number of laws such as the Health and Safety Act. As an employee this duty is 'to take reasonable care for the health and safety of ... [yourself] ... and of others who may be affected by ... [your] ... acts or omissions at work'. Your duty is not to ensure that no harm will ever occur, but a duty to take reasonable care to avoid harm happening to others (Unison, 2003).

2. As well as having a duty to take reasonable care to avoid injury or harm to the person you support you also have a duty to enable them to achieve and maintain the maximum possible level of independence, choice and control. To live the life they choose and to achieve their dreams and aspirations. You have a duty to support the person to take control of their life and make informed choices about the support they receive (GSCC *Code of practice for social care workers* 2001 and *Enabling risks, ensuring safety: self directed support and personal budgets*, SCIE, 2010).

Balancing these two aspects of the duty of care is the challenge that you and all social care workers have in supporting people with a learning disability to lead a fulfilling life.

In relation to your job, write down a list of:

- *all of the people you think you owe a duty of care to;*
- *all of those that you think you do not owe a duty of care to.*

Discuss your lists with your manager and the duty of care you owe each person.

DUTY OF CARE

| Protection from harm | | Promoting independence, choice and control |

The balance to consider when thinking about duty of care.

The Social Care Councils for the four UK nations all have a *Code of practice for social care workers* (see the end of this chapter for details). You should be using the Code of Practice for your country to inform how you work. The Codes of Practice make it clear in their standards that you should be considering these tensions between rights and choice and preventing harm in your day to day work. They say that you should:

- *support service users' rights to control their lives and make informed choices about the services they receive;*

- *recognise that service users have the right to take risks and help them to identify and manage potential and actual risk to themselves and others*

- *take necessary steps to minimise the risk to service users from doing actual or potential harm to themselves or other people.*

As a support worker you owe a duty of care to the people you support, to their family carers as well as to the colleagues you work with. If you work in a particular building such as a day centre or residential home you also have a duty of care to any visitors to the building. This means that if you were thoughtless or neglectful in your work these are the people who would be most likely to be harmed.

Why is a duty of care important?

Duty of care is important because you have both a legal or statutory and a moral responsibility in your role as a learning disability worker. A legal duty means that you need to work in a certain way in order to comply with particular laws: for example the Health and Safety at Work Act, the Mental Capacity Act and the Human Rights Act.

A moral or ethical duty means you need to provide support in a particular way as a social care worker because it is the right and fair thing to do. As a social care worker you need to work to agreed values and principles. These are set out in the Code of Practice and in the values, aims and objectives of your organisation.

A legal duty of care

We all have a common law duty of care to each other as set out in a legal judgement from 80 years ago. This judgement said that, *you must take reasonable care to avoid acts or omissions which you can reasonably foresee would be likely to injure your neighbour.* This judgement goes on to say that your 'neighbour' is a person who is so closely or directly affected by your act that you ought reasonably have thoughts about them being affected by your act or omission. (This ruling comes from Lord Atkin in the case of Donoghue v Stevenson, in 1932.)

This ruling on our common law duty of care emphasises that whether we are at work or not, every one of us needs to take reasonable care to avoid acts or omissions which we can reasonably foresee are likely to injure another person.

In addition to this common law duty of care employers and employees have specific legal rights and duties. For example, the Health and Safety at Work Act 1974 sets out the employee's duty: 'to take reasonable care for the health and safety of himself (herself) and of others who may be affected by his (her) acts or omissions at work'.

In particular the Health and Safety at Work Act 1974 gives a legal responsibility to any employer. This could be a care organisation or an individual who is employing a personal assistant. The Act says the following: 'It shall be the responsibility of every employer to ensure, so far as is reasonably practicable, the health, safety and welfare of all his employees'.

The employer needs to make sure that everything they do seeks to reduce the risks of any incident occurring that might cause death, injury, physical harm, and trauma or abuse, loss of property or damage to relationships or reputation.

As an employee of either a care organisation or an individual, this means you have a duty of care to:

- work safely and efficiently;

- use all necessary equipment safely;

- use protective equipment when necessary;

- report any incidents that may lead to or have led to injury;

- follow carefully any agreed procedures or agreed ways of working;

- assist in the investigation of any accident so that any risk of harm can be reduced in the future.

(Taken from *Supporting safely. A guide for individuals receiving support and their families and friends* from www.in-control.org.uk)

For more information about health and safety in social care work see the *Health and safety for learning disability workers* book in this series.

In law if you fail in your duty of care as a support worker in the areas above then you might be accused of negligence. This means that your support in a particular situation fell below the minimum standard expected by your employer. It also means that you did not do what a reasonable person would do to protect an individual from harm.

In the story of Peter at the beginning of this chapter, Louise has a legal duty of care towards him as he lives in the residential home where she works and he is supported by her and her colleagues. In her work Louise must ensure that what she does causes no harm to Peter, the other people living in the home, her colleagues and family carers and others who visit the home. It is her responsibility to see that where possible, Peter does not come to any harm as a result of her actions or her failure to carry out a task. Louise has a legal duty to ensure that she follows all the health and safety training and information she has been given, for example in relation to using equipment or handling hazardous substances. She must report any health and safety concerns and also request training if she is asked to do something that she has not been trained to do, such as administering medication or using a particular hoist.

If you are a learning disability worker who supports people in their own homes, in the community or in supported employment, you also have a legal duty of care to the person you support as well as to your colleagues.

A moral or ethical duty of care

In your job as a learning disability worker you need to work to a clear set of values and principles. These values and principles inform the moral or ethical duty of care that you have. They are set out in a number of places such as:

- the Code of Practice;
- the Skills for Care *Common core principles to support self* care (from www.skillsforcare.org.uk);
- your employer's vision, aims and objectives;
- the Dignity Challenge (from www.dignityincare.org.uk

The Code of Practice says social care workers must:

- Protect the rights and promote the interests of service users and carers.
- Strive to establish and maintain the trust and confidence of service users and carers.
- Promote the independence of service users while protecting them as far as possible from danger or harm.
- Respect the rights of service users whilst seeking to ensure that their behaviour does not harm themselves or other people.
- Uphold public trust and confidence in social care services.
- Be accountable for the quality of their work and take responsibility for maintaining and improving their knowledge and skills.

Duty of care in your role

Activity

Talk to your line manager about the values of the organisation that you work for. For each of the values identify one way that you can demonstrate that value to underpin your duty of care.

In relation to your duty of care the Code of Practice says *you must strive to establish and maintain the trust and confidence* of people with a learning disability and their family carers by:

2.1 being honest and trustworthy;

2.2 communicating in an appropriate, open, accurate and straightforward way;

2.3 respecting confidential information;

2.4 being reliable and dependable;

2.5 honouring work commitments and agreements;

You have a duty to communicate in an appropriate, open, accurate and straightforward way.

2.6 declaring issues that might create a conflict of interest;

2.7 adhering to policies and procedures.

Activity

Talk to your colleagues about the values and principles that underpin your work. Look at the Dignity Challenge or the Common Core Principles and decide as a team how you demonstrate these values in practice.

Managing risk and duty of care

Thinking point

Think about some of the experiences in your life where you have chosen to take a risk to do something. How did you decide whether the risk was acceptable?

Risk is part of everyday life for all of us. There are risks in day-to-day activities such as cooking a meal, crossing the road, going out to visit friends. There are even risks if we choose to stay in bed all day. Managing risks together with the person you support, their family carers, your colleagues and manager is an important part of understanding duty of care.

For example, at the beginning of this chapter Marie, Amina's key worker, in the example probably recognised that there are risks of cuts and burns involved in supporting Amina to learn to prepare her breakfast. However, with good preparation and support, the risks may be worth taking so that Amina is more independent and has more choices. Your duty of care, in a situation like this, is to identify both the gains and the possible risks in an activity and then work in partnership with others to reduce the risks. This approach to duty of care means you are balancing the potential gains of more independence for Amina with the possibility of harm and how you can reduce that harm.

Risk is part of everyday life.

Here is a list of activities that you might be supporting a person with learning disabilities to do.

- Eating and drinking.

- Travelling on a bus to visit friends at a cafe.

- Doing voluntary work at a local plant nursery.

- Making a drink or snack.

- Going to a community activity they enjoy, e.g. bingo, church, the fishing club.

In every situation your duty of care is to take all reasonable steps to avoid or reduce the risk of harm to the person while at the same time promoting their independence and choices. Where there are a number of ways which would reduce the risk of harm, you must choose the one which lets the person with learning disabilities maintain their independence as much as possible. Part of your job is to discuss with the person involved, their family carers, and your colleagues how you can provide support that will increase choice and independence while reducing the risk of harm.

Duty of care and the safeguarding and protecting of people with a learning disability

The first priority should always be to ensure the safety and protection of vulnerable adults. To this end it is the responsibility of all staff to act on any suspicions of abuse or neglect.

DH and Home Office, 2000.

Safeguarding people with a learning disability involves a range of activities including upholding the person's right to be safe at the same time as respecting their right to make choices. As we have seen throughout this chapter these tensions are part of your day-to-day work.

As a learning disability worker, safeguarding is the duty that you have to make sure that the person or people that you support are not abused or neglected. The people with a learning disability you support have a right to live their life, with the support they need, free from abuse, neglect or negligence. You should observe the following:

- Make sure that you know about the different types of abuse and how to recognise that a person is being abused. Safeguarding training should be part of your induction in the first few weeks of your employment. Listen carefully to any complaints or concerns about abuse that are brought to your notice by the person you support, a family carer, colleague or member of the public.
- Always report any concerns in line with the policies of your organisation. Discuss how you would report a disclosure of abuse with your line manager if you don't know what to do.
- Know about the policies and procedures in your organisation for reporting disclosure of abuse or concerns relating to abuse and neglect.
- Make sure that the people you support and their family carers know about different types of abuse and how to report any concerns.

For additional information on safeguarding and protection see the *Principles of safeguarding and protection for learning disability workers* book in this series.

If you are a personal assistant employed directly by a person with a learning disability or their family you also have a duty of care to prevent the abuse or neglect of the person you support. Although your employer may not have the same policies and procedures as you might find in a care organisation, they should still tell you about abuse and how to report any concerns that you may have. If you are in any doubt about what to do, get in touch with your local authority's adult protection team.

Remember that most types of abuse are criminal offences. For more information on staying safe for people with a direct payment or individual budget, look at *Supporting safely. A guide for individuals receiving support and their families and friends* from www.in-control.org.uk

Key points from this chapter

In Chapter 1 we have looked at what duty of care means. In summary it includes the following:

- Avoid acts or omissions that may cause harm to others.
- Promote the rights, independence and choices of the people you support.
- Always work to a clear set of values.
- Be aware of how to report any concerns about abuse or neglect.

References and where to go for more information

References

GSCC (2001) *Code of Practice for Social Care Workers* from www.gscc.org.uk

Healthcare Commission (2006) *Joint Investigation into the Provision of Services for People with Learning Disabilities at Cornwall Partnership NHS Trust.* London: Healthcare Commission

Healthcare Commission (2007) *An Investigation into the Services for People with Learning Disabilities at Sutton and Merton Primary Care Trust.* London: Healthcare Commission

In Control (2009) *Supporting Safely. A guide for individuals receiving support and their families and friends* from www.in-control.org.uk

SCIE (2010) *Enabling Risks, Ensuring Safety: Self directed support and personal budgets* from www.scie.org.uk

Skills for Care and Skills for Health (2008) *Common Core Principles to Support Self Care – a guide to support implementation.* London and Leeds. From www.skillsforcare.org.uk *or* www.skillsforhealth.org.uk

The Dignity Challenge – *a clear statement of what people can expect from a service that respects dignity.* Details available from www.scie.org.uk *and* www.dignityincare.org.uk/DignityCareCampaign

Unison (2003) *The Duty of Care: A handbook to assist healthcare staff carrying out their duty of care to patients, colleagues and themselves.* London: Unison

Websites

The Social Care Councils (responsible for the regulation and registration of Social Workers and other Social Care Workers) are:

General Social Care Council (England) www.gscc.org.uk
Care Council for Wales www.ccwales.org.uk
Scottish Social Services Council www.sssc.uk.com
Northern Ireland Social Care Council www.niscc.info

Chapter 2

Dilemmas that may arise about duty of care

Every day Stuart makes choices about his life. He chooses his food, the clothes he wants to wear and what he does day to day. This particular day he came out of his bedroom in his favourite heavy winter coat with a hat and scarf and gloves as well. The only problem was it was one of the hottest days in July. I talked to Stuart and suggested he may be too hot in those clothes to go to the supermarket for the weekly shop. But he insisted this is what he wanted to wear.

Sometimes the staff at the supermarket are friendly and understanding. But when he gets excited and loud, people can get a bit scared of him. Sometimes people stare at Stuart and I get angry and upset for him. I thought Stuart might be treated badly at the supermarket dressed up in his winter clothes and would be a source of ridicule so thought it would be best we didn't go out. But Stuart really wanted to go out to get his Dad's birthday card and present. I was in a dilemma and if I wasn't careful this could lead to a conflict between me and Stuart.

Becky, Stuart's personal assistant

Introduction

Every day is different when you work with people with a learning disability. Some days things go smoothly and the person you support has a good day and achieves the outcomes they want. Other days can include conflicts and dilemmas and then you may need to ask what is your duty of care to the person you support in a particular situation. As a learning disability worker you need to be aware of the potential dilemmas that might arise in your work situation between the rights of the person you support and your duty of care. Thinking ahead and knowing where and when some of these conflicts or dilemmas might occur is important, as by being prepared you might well be able to avoid potential conflicts before they happen. In particular you need to get to know the person you support well. You also need to know what you can and cannot do in such a situation and where to go for advice.

Learning outcomes

This chapter will help you to:

- understand the potential dilemmas that may arise between your duty of care and a person's rights;

- describe how to manage risk associated with conflicts or dilemmas;

- know about your role in managing conflicts and dilemmas;

- understand where to get additional support and advice in relation to dilemmas in your work.

This chapter covers:

Common Induction Standards – Standard 5 – Principles for implementing duty of care: Learning Outcome 2

Level 2 HSC 24 – Introduction to duty of care: Learning Outcome 2

Level 3 HSC 34 – Principles for implementing duty of care: Learning Outcome 2

The potential dilemmas that may arise between a person's rights and your duty of care

Activity

Think of a person you support and some of the dilemmas and conflicts that may arise between the person's rights and your duty of care. Write down three potential conflicts or dilemmas and discuss with your manager why you think the dilemmas might occur.

Dilemmas and conflicts can arise in a number of situations, including when:

- organisations and workers are particularly concerned about possible risks (this means people with learning disabilities are prevented from learning new skills, developing new relationships or taking part in new activities);

- a person is frustrated because they are not offered choices or given information in a suitable format for them to make decisions;

- a worker is asked by their manager to do something they are not trained to do;

- the wishes of the person are in conflict with what their family carers think is best for them;

- a person who has capacity to make a decision makes an unwise decision that the worker finds hard to accept or support;

- family carers are not listened to and their knowledge and experience are not considered and used to inform the support required for their relative;

- the actions or behaviours of one person have a negative impact on other people in the same setting;

- there is a lack of sufficient support and a person is put at risk as a result.

Duty of care is a balancing act between reducing the possibility of harm and enabling choice.

In the conflicts and dilemmas you have identified and those in the list above you need to consider the impact on the person and on their rights. When you are faced with a conflict or dilemma you may find it useful to think about a number of questions.

- What harm might the person come to in this situation? Will it have an impact on other people?

- What does the person's person-centred plan or support plan tell you that might help in the situation?

- Has a risk assessment been carried out, or should one be carried out?

- Are there any adult protection issues involved?

- What rights do all the people involved in the situation have?

- What policies and procedures should you be checking with that might tell you what to do?

- Who can you ask for advice and information?

Remember that as a new worker supporting people with a learning disability you don't need to manage the conflicts or dilemmas that you face alone. You should seek support from your manager, more experienced colleagues or, where appropriate, family carers who can help you think through how you should respond.

Supporting rights

When thinking about the rights of people with a learning disability these are clearly set out in recent legislations and policies, for example in the:

- Human Rights Act (1998);

- Equality Act (2010);

- Mental Capacity Act (2005).

Remember when considering dilemmas and conflicts that according to the European Convention on Human Rights and the Human Rights Act (1998) you, the person with a learning disability that you support and their family carers have the same human rights. The rights that people with a learning disability tell us are most important to them are:

- the right to life;

- freedom from torture and degrading treatment;

- the right to respect for private and family life;

- the right to marry and to start a family;

- the right not to be discriminated against in respect of these rights and freedoms;

- the right to peaceful enjoyment of your property.

It is these rights and freedoms that you should be upholding and protecting in your day-to-day work with people with a learning disability and their families. You will find out more information on rights and recent policies and laws in the *Equality and inclusion for learning disability workers* and the *Introduction to supporting people with a learning disability* books in this series.

Protecting people from harm

Often dilemmas and conflicts occur when there is an imbalance between rights and protecting people from harm. In some situations this can be when an organisation and its staff find risk taking difficult and as a consequence overprotect people. For example, a recent investigation by the Healthcare Commission (2007) into a learning disability service in Sutton and Merton noted that delivery was very poor care and:

> ... there was a fear of taking therapeutic risks in the approach to care in the learning disability service that to some extent prevented the development of new skills in people with learning disabilities ... This in turn meant that there were many breaches of people's human rights.

This quote shows the importance of supporting people to take risks that have been carefully assessed, as failing to do so can breach their human rights.

As well as promoting a person's rights and choices, you also have to consider your duty of care. This is your responsibility to take due care in order to protect people from unnecessary risk of harm. This includes the person's psychological and physical safety.

So let us look back to the example of Stuart and Becky at the beginning of this chapter. The table below goes through the questions that you could use when facing similar conflicts or dilemmas.

Issues to consider	Stuart and Becky's example
What harm might the person come to in this situation? Will it have an impact on other people?	Stuart might get too hot and feel uncomfortable in his winter clothes. This could make him more agitated at the shops. His behaviour may cause people to stare at him or call him names. Becky may feel anxious and be unsure how to react. There is a risk that, because of the heat and the reaction of others, Stuart's behaviour may become more challenging.
What does the person's person centred plan or support plan tell you that might help in the situation?	Stuart's plan gives lots of detail about how to offer him choices that Becky could have used when supporting him to decide on clothes. The plan also gives information on how to support Stuart when he is agitated. Using the information in the plan could have helped Becky prevent the dilemma arising in the first place.
Has a risk assessment been carried out, or should one be done?	A behaviour support plan together with risk assessments had been produced by Stuart's mum, who manages his direct payment. Becky needs to be familiar with these to help her provide good day-to-day support.
Are there any adult protection issues involved?	No immediate issues.
What rights and choices do all the people involved in the situation have?	Stuart has the right to self-expression through choosing his clothes. He has a right to family life; celebrating his dad's birthday is important to him.
What policies and procedures should you be checking with that might tell you what to do?	Stuart's support is managed through a direct payment. Becky and the other personal assistants are employed by Stuart and his mum. They don't have policies and procedures but they do have agreed ways of working. All the personal assistants need to work to Stuart's support plan and be familiar with the detailed behaviour support plan.

Issues to consider	Stuart and Becky's example
Who can you ask for advice and information?	Becky could talk to Stuart's mum, who manages his direct payment, about the dilemma and how she would have managed the situation. After the issue is resolved Becky could reflect on the day to explore what she has learnt and how she might manage a similar situation in the future.

Activity

Now go back to the activity at the beginning of this chapter and look at one of the dilemmas or conflicts that you identified. Use the questions in the table above to consider how you might manage the dilemma. Discuss your ideas with your line manager.

Managing risks associated with conflicts or dilemmas

Every day we take risks. Crossing the road and driving a car are high risk activities. Even making a cup of tea or cooking a meal involves risks. Imagine your life then if you took away anything that involved taking a risk. It would be a very boring life. Unfortunately this is the experience of many people with learning disabilities because the people supporting them are seeking to protect them from everyday risks.

In our day-to-day life we are often carrying out informal risk assessments without consciously thinking that this is what we are doing. For example, when deciding whether to:

- pull out on a roundabout in front of a lorry;

- walk down a dark alley at night;

- climb up a ladder to repair a drain pipe.

Very occasionally if a situation seems to be more risky or dangerous we might talk through possible risks with a member of our family or a friend before doing something like a parachute jump for charity.

Your duty of care might conflict with the rights of the person to take risks when:

- the person is in a situation in which he or she is being exploited or abused by others;
- the person is at serious risk of harming themselves or other people;
- the person has a serious mental health illness which is a risk to them or others;
- a situation has deteriorated to a point that the person is unable to retrieve it and requires support to do so;
- a possible criminal charge is involved.

When you work supporting people with a learning disability, carrying out a more formal risk assessment may be useful in helping you, your colleagues and the person's family carers to be aware of your duty of care.

Carrying out risk assessments can help you work through what the risk is, what the severity of the risk is, who may be affected by the risk and what you can do to minimise those risks. Risk assessments can help you to find a balance between an individual's rights and protection. It can help you come up with ideas that can reduce the risk.

Activity

Does your service have a risk assessment or risk management policy? If so, read it carefully. Does it have risk assessment forms for completion? Talk to your line manager about risk management and your role in managing risks with the people you support.

A risk assessment is a careful examination of what could cause harm to a person in a particular situation. Your employer needs to undertake risk assessments to ensure the safety of their workers, for example relating to lone working or using particular equipment. In social care work with people with a learning disability, risk assessments are also used to examine any risks associated with the person's support. A good risk assessment will identify and uphold the person's rights and will help avoid injury and ill health.

RISK ASSESSMENT FORM

Identify the risks or risks that might occur

Describe the risk

How likely is it that the risk will happen

What impact will it have on the person and others

How might the risk be managed

Completed by   -

Signed   -

Date   -

Know about your role in managing conflicts and dilemmas

As a new worker supporting people with a learning disability you will not always know what your duty of care is in every situation. You will feel better able to deal with conflicts and dilemmas as you complete your induction and undertake further training. In any situation you need to be clear what your role is and what the limits of your responsibility are. To understand what your role is in relation to duty of care dilemmas, you will find it helpful to carry out the following:

- Read your job description and contract of employment. If you have any questions discuss them with your manager. Are you clear about your responsibilities?

- Familiarise yourself with the policies and procedures of your organisation, or if you are employed as a personal assistant by a person with a learning disability or their family, the agreed ways of working.

- Get to know the person you support well by spending time with them and reading their person centred plan or support plan.

- Use your supervision sessions with your line manager to clarify your role and what your duty of care is in particular situations.

Where to get additional support and advice in relation to dilemmas in your work

Activity

Go back to the list of conflicts and dilemmas that you identified in the first activity in this chapter. For each of the three examples, think about what your role is. Where you would go to for support and advice? Talk through your ideas with your line manager.

When you experience conflicts or dilemmas relating to your duty of care there are a number of places you can go to for additional support and advice, including:

There are a number of people you can get support from when you are faced with a conflict or dilemma.

- your line manager and other senior colleagues in your organisation;

- the person you support and their person-centred plan or support plan;

- the family carers of the person you support, who often know them best and can advise on how similar situations may have been handled in the past;

- the person's advocate if they have one;

- the policies and procedures of your organisation;

- the laws and policies that relate to rights and duty of care.

Key points from this chapter

- There can be tensions between the person's rights and your duty of care.

- Getting to know the person and their person centred plan is important.

- Effective risk assessment can help you manage conflicts and dilemmas.

- Take time to assess situations positively, working out ways to minimise risks.

- If you need advice about a dilemma in your workplace you should talk to your line manager or a senior colleague, and look in the policies and procedures for your organisation.

References and where to go for more information

References

Healthcare Commission (2006) *Joint Investigation into the Provision of Services for People with Learning Disabilities at Cornwall Partnership NHS Trust.* London: Healthcare Commission

Healthcare Commission (2007) *An Investigation into the Services for People with Learning Disabilities at Sutton and Merton Primary Care Trust.* London: Healthcare Commission

Joint Parliamentary Committee on Human Rights (2008) *A Life Like Any Other? Human rights of adults with a learning disability* available from www.parliament.uk

Legislation, policies and reports

All UK legislation can be downloaded from www.legislation.gov.uk

Policies and reports for Northern Ireland, Scotland and Wales can be found at www.northernireland.gov.uk www.scotland.gov.uk and www.wales.gov.uk respectively. Policies and reports for England can be found on the website of the relevant government department.

Equality Act (2010)

Health and Safety at Work Act (1974)

Human Rights Act (1998)

Mental Capacity Act (2005)

Websites

Health and Safety Executive www.hse.gov.uk

Chapter 3

Handling comments, complaints, adverse events and incidents

You can tell someone in authority or a parent, but you are not often taken seriously or believed ... It's hard to get people to listen ... it's hard to make a complaint about someone you know – they might take it out on you ... I know where the forms are but not what to do with them ... It can be embarrassing to complain ... It is hard to complain about people because it might get them into trouble ... It is important to know who to talk to, if you don't it is very difficult to complain ... You need to be able to trust someone ...

Comments made by people with learning disabilities in evidence to the Joint Parliamentary Committee on Human Rights, from *A Life Like Any Other? Human rights of adults with learning disabilities, 2008*

Introduction

Complaining is something that is difficult for many people irrespective of their abilities or disabilities. Many of us simply 'suffer in silence' rather than face the possible stress or embarrassment of making a complaint.

The quotations above are taken from evidence by people with a learning disability to a parliamentary inquiry and clearly show that people with a learning disability often experience difficulties in making a complaint and having it taken seriously. Family carers similarly tell of some of the difficulties they experience in either commenting on good support or making a complaint.

Most care providers seek to encourage feedback both good and bad on the support they provide and have a compliments and complaints process to ensure a consistent approach. As a social care worker you have a duty *to help service users and carers to make complaints, taking complaints seriously and responding to them or passing them to the appropriate person (GSCC Code* of Practice, 2001). In this chapter we look at your role in supporting people to make complaints and knowing what you should do when handling a comment or complaint. This chapter also covers recognising and handling adverse events, incidents and near misses.

Learning outcomes

This chapter will help you to:

- explain why it is important that individuals know how to make a complaint;

- explain the main points of agreed procedures for handling complaints;

- describe your role in responding to complaints as part of your duty of care;

- know how to recognise and respond to accidents, incidents, errors and near misses.

This chapter covers:

- Common Induction Standards – Standard 5 – Principles for implementing duty of care: Learning Outcomes 3 and 4

- Level 2 SHC 24 – Introduction to duty of care: Learning Outcome 3

- Level 3 SHC 34 – Principles for implementing duty of care: Learning Outcome 3

Why it is important that individuals know how to make a complaint

What is a complaint? A complaint is defined by the National Audit Office (2008) as 'an expression of dissatisfaction, disquiet or discontent about actions, decisions or apparent failings of a service provision which requires a response'.

We all have the right to accessible and adequate complaints procedures. In particular the right we have to a fair, timely and independent hearing of our complaint is of utmost importance.

The investigations in poor services and abuse in Cornwall in 2006, Sutton and Merton in 2007, and the *Death by Indifference* report published in 2007, are sad reminders of the potential for abuse, neglect and infringement of human rights that can result when people's voices go unheard. People who rely on services are also those who face the biggest barriers to being heard. They rely on others, including friends, family carers, advocates and other people who support them, to ensure their right to complain, including accessing complaints procedures, is upheld.

In 1995 Ken Simons looked at complaints and people with learning disabilities. He pointed out that it is harder to complain when:

- you are vulnerable due to stress, illness, inexperience or lack of knowledge;
- you have difficulty expressing your views;
- there is a big status gap between you and those you complain about;
- those you complain about have continuing power over you;
- you are isolated.

Ken Simons found that:

- most people with learning disabilities thought the idea of complaining was probably good but tended to stick to 'safe' subjects such as cold food;
- a few people with learning disabilities thought complaining was bad – some thought it was not possible to question staff;
- people with learning disabilities were not always clear about whom to complain to and lacked knowledge about complaints procedures;
- there was fear of the consequences of complaining.

Since this time most services have tried to make their complaints processes more accessible, for example using videos to provide information on how to complain. Many local services have developed a range of easy-read complaint leaflets in an attempt to make complaint procedures understandable. You can find a list of some of these resources in the BILD report *Hearing from the Seldom Heard*.

As a learning disability worker part of your role is to try to address this. It is vital that people with learning disabilities have access to a complaints procedure that they can understand and that responds to them.

However, there is considerable evidence that many people with learning disabilities still find it difficult to make complaints. People with learning disabilities have reported a number of feelings and thoughts when talking about complaining.

> Make out you are the important one, but not really

> Dusted under the carpet

> Staff don't listen

> Not allowed to use the complaint procedure

> Cannot read the complaint form

> Called a trouble maker

> They thought it was trivial but it was important to me

People with learning disabilities have reported a number of thoughts about complaining

Having an accessible complaints policy and a listening culture will make it easier for people to report a compliment or complaint.

People with learning disabilities face many barriers in being able to complain about the services they receive. *A Life Like Any Other?* (2008) said that may be because:

- the complaints system is confusing and difficult to understand;

- some people do not have the confidence to complain;

- people with complex needs cannot complain because people don't know how to communicate with them.

The BILD materials *Hearing from the Seldom Heard* identified some good practice recommendations for supporting people with learning disabilities to have their concerns heard. Although the recommendations were for people with complex communication needs, they apply to all people with learning disabilities. The recommendations are for support workers to:

1. **Get to know the person you support really well** so you can see things as far as possible from their point of view and spot when they may be unhappy. This clearly links into good person-centred working.

2. **Learn to communicate better** with the person you support – a recurring theme which underpins any good practice in supporting people with learning disabilities (see *The BILD Guide: Communication is a human right*).

3. **Raise awareness of the human rights of people with a learning disability** including the right to complain, both among people with learning disabilities and those who support and care for them.

4. **Enable access to appropriate advocacy** such as citizen and non-instructed advocacy for all who are unable to represent their own views and feelings easily. Non-instructed advocacy is for people who are not able to instruct an advocate independently, for example, someone with a profound and complex learning disability.

5. **Enable access to complaints buddies** – a complaints buddy is somebody who can look out for the person and take action on their behalf. This could well be a family member, but it might also be a friend, a person with learning disabilities, or a paid worker. Complaining is often a difficult thing to do on your own and people with learning disabilities should have the support and practical assistance of a complaints buddy. A complaints buddy can either support the person with learning disabilities to complain or act on their behalf.

6. **Make sure people know about the complaints policy** – check that the person or people you support, as well as their family carers and friends, know how to complain and that they have the information in a way that suits their communication.

You can read more examples of good practice in supporting people with making comments or complaints in the BILD materials *Hearing from the Seldom Heard*.

Hearing from the
Seldom Heard

**Supporting complaints from people with learning disabilities
and complex communication needs**

The good practice recommendations

1. Getting to know people really well

2. Learning to communicate better

3. Raising awareness of human rights

4. Access to appropriate advocacy

5. Access to complaints buddies

6. Making effective use of complaints procedures

The Department of Health has provided funding for this project

An example of good practice recommendations for supporting people with learning disabilities to have their concerns heard.

The procedures for handling a complaint

Activity

Find out and read your organisation's compliments and complaints policy. Then talk to your line manager about:

- *what you should do if you receive a complaint;*
- *how you might support a person to make a complaint who has indicated that they are unhappy with the care they are receiving.*

The ideal situation is that any complaint will be resolved as quickly as possible and also informally – this means without involving unions or external bodies.

Here are some of the main points to follow when dealing with complaints.

- Listen carefully to what the person is telling you.

- Keep accurate records of all communication that takes place regarding the complaint.

- Keep the person who makes the complaint informed at all times.

- Make sure all the points raised by the complaint are responded to.

- Make sure the complaint is handled quickly and tell the person who has made the complaint how long it will take.

Listen carefully if someone comes to you with a compliment or complaint and keep a record of what is said.

How to respond to complaints

Thinking point

If a family carer, member of the public or a person you support made a complaint to you, do you know what you should do?

It is important, if a person makes a complaint to you, that you acknowledge the complaint and you don't ignore or dismiss what they tell you, regardless of your own views. Sometimes a person may just want to feel they are being listened to.

Often after the initial incident that causes the complaint is resolved the complaint is withdrawn. Regardless of the seriousness of the complaint it is vital that it is handled with sensitivity from the beginning and that it is handled in line with the organisation's policies and procedures.

It is important that you act professionally at all times regarding the complaint. Make sure you listen carefully and are clear about what the complaint is. If someone approaches you to make a complaint it may be useful to take them into a private room so that the nature of the complaint and the details remain confidential. It may be useful to make some notes about what the person is saying. As well as making notes you need to ask the person if they need support to put their complaint in writing.

Once you have received the complaint it is important that you then follow the complaints policy and procedures for your organisation. Although it can be hard to be immediately involved in a complaint it is important that both your organisation and the people mentioned in a complaint use it as a learning opportunity. Complaints can provide an opportunity to develop personally and in your work and it can be useful to think about it as a learning opportunity. Remember you have a duty of care to the individuals you support and if you are failing in that duty of care it is important that you address this. Also, the complaint can be a warning that the organisation you work for needs to change or update the way they work, to reflect better practice. A complaint can be used to assess, plan, implement and evaluate our actions. Remember the reports mentioned earlier and the importance of taking complaints seriously. If not, people could be mistreated or abused or poor practice might continue.

Recognising and handling adverse events, accidents, incidents and near misses

Even in the best managed service, things can go wrong. This can also happen when people manage their own support and directly employ personal assistants. While accepting that workers are accountable for their actions, most employers would not want to encourage a blame culture that exposes or punishes workers. Instead most organisations want to learn from any accidents, near misses or incidents so that the quality of support for people with a learning disability and their family carers can improve and potential risks be avoided. This means that as a learning disability worker you need to know what to do in the case of an accident, incident or near miss as this is part of your duty of care. Hopefully you will never be confronted by such a situation, but being prepared is important so that you know what to do, just in case.

Definitions

An accident is an undesired or unintended event which results in physical or psychological harm to an individual, damage to property or goods or the environment. Examples could include:

- a car accident when you are travelling with a person with a learning disability;
- a trip or fall when out;
- dropping cleaning chemicals that cause burns to your leg.

An adverse event is an unanticipated problem involving risk to a person that results in harm to them or others. This could include an injury requiring medical treatment, as in the following examples.

- Because of train delays you are late home with the person you support and they take their medication two hours late. This makes them sick.
- Forgetting to take an inhaler on a day out and the person gets wheezy.
- Two workers phone in sick and there are not enough staff in the home to support everyone to get up. The bank workers arrive very late and one person whose behaviour is sometimes challenging lashes out because he is bored and not doing what he planned to do, and he hurts another resident.

An incident is any event that could have led or did lead to unintended or unexpected harm, loss or damage, e.g. theft, fire, violence, abuse, ill health or infection. For example, this could include:

- a person getting lost on a group visit to a theme park;
- theft of vital health equipment from the person's home;
- a person being threatened by a neighbour;
- the boiler exploding in a home or day centre.

An error is an action that doesn't go as planned, or when a wrong judgement or decision is made that leads to physical or psychological harm. For example:

- a support worker fails to secure a person's wheelchair properly in their car and they are injured when going round a corner;
- a new worker wrongly administers a person's medication.

A near miss is when something that could go wrong is identified and prevented and so did not result in injury, illness, or damage – but it had the potential to do so. For example:

- when lifting a person using a hoist the equipment failed but thanks to the quick reaction of the support workers the person was gently lowered without any injury.

Thinking point

Have you any experience of an accident, near miss or adverse incident in your work supporting people with a learning disability?

What could cause a near miss or adverse incident in your work situation?

Some accidents and incidents that occur at work need to be reported under the Reporting of Incidents, Diseases and Dangerous Occurrences Regulations (RIDDOR) 1995. Accidents and incidents reportable under RIDDOR are:

- those that result in a major injury;

- specific dangerous occurrences;

- specific diseases.

When you report an accident, near miss or incident your line manager will be able to advise you whether it needs to be reported to the Health and Safety Executive under the RIDDOR system. You will also learn more about reporting in the *Health and safety for learning disability workers* book in this series and in any health and safety training you attend.

Policies and procedures

Most social care and health organisations have policies and procedures relating to reporting and managing accidents, incidents and near misses. These are in place to make sure that the people who use the service, their family carers and workers can alert the organisation to any issues that if left unattended could lead to serious risk or injury. Workers must report using the policies and procedures so that the organisation:

- meets its legal requirements;

- ensures the safety of people who use the organisation;

- takes appropriate action to manage poor practice;

- is proactive in anticipating possible dangers;

- can learn from past incidents and improve practice.

Find your organisation's policy on reporting accidents, incidents and near misses and read it. Find the answers to these questions.

1. *What should you do when you are involved in an accident, adverse incident or near miss?*
2. *How and where should you record information about what happened?*
3. *Where does the information go and what happens to it?*

At your next supervision talk to your manager about the policy and procedure and if you have any questions or concerns make sure you know exactly what you should do.

Your role in relation to adverse events, accidents, incidents and near misses

As you learnt in Chapters 1 and 2 in this book, you have a duty of care to the people you support and your colleagues to take reasonable steps to ensure that you reduce the risk of harm to them. This duty extends to ensuring that wherever possible you avoid any accidents, incidents and near misses. In addition your role is to do the following.

It is important to read and follow your organisation's policies and procedures in relation to accidents or incidents.

- Make sure you have received the necessary health and safety training for your job and any additional training that you need to work safely.
- Make sure that you have read and understand the person-centred plan or support plan of the person or people you support so that you are aware of any potential risks or risk management plans.
- Know and follow the policies and procedure of your organisation in relation to accidents, incidents and near misses and if you have any questions or concerns ask your line manager for further information.

References and where to go for more information

References

BILD (2008) *Hearing from the Seldom Heard* downloadable from http://www.bild.org.uk/humanrights_seldomheard.htm

Healthcare Commission (2006) *Joint Investigation into the Provision of Services for People with Learning Disabilities at Cornwall Partnership NHS Trust.* London: Healthcare Commission

Healthcare Commission (2007) *An Investigation into the Services for People with Learning Disabilities at Sutton and Merton Primary Care Trust.* London: Healthcare Commission

Joint Parliamentary Committee on Human Rights (2008) *A life like any other? Human Rights of Adults with Learning Disabilities,* available from www.parliament.uk

Mencap (2007) *Death by Indifference: Following up the Treat Me Right! Report.* Mencap: London

Michael, Sir Jonathan (2008) *Healthcare for All – Independent Inquiry into Access to Healthcare for People with Learning Disabilities,* from www.oldt.nhs.uk/documents/Healthcareforall.pdf

National Audit Office (2008) *Feeding back? Learning from Complaints Handling in Health and Social Care.* London: National Audit Office

Simons, K (1995) *I'm not complaining: The right to complain: Making complaints procedures work for people with learning difficulties,* in Philpott T and Ward L (eds) (1995) *Values and Visions. Changing ideas in services for people with learning difficulties.* Oxford: Butterworth Heinemann

Thurman, Sue (2009) *BILD Guide: Making Complaints Work for People with Learning Disabilities.* Kidderminster BILD

Websites

Organisations that can help with complaints

Independent Complaints Advocacy Service (ICAS) provides independent support to people wishing to complain about treatment in the NHS. Three providers deliver ICAS in different parts of the country:

The Carers' Federation: www.carersfederation.co.uk

POhWER: www.pohwer.net

SEAP: www.seap.org.uk

The Patient Advice and Liaison Service (PALS) www.pals.nhs.uk is an NHS service which helps to resolve concerns or problems when using the NHS.

The Parliamentary and Health Ombudsman www.ombudsman.org.uk carries out independent investigations into complaints about UK government departments and the NHS in England in order to help improve public services.

For more information on making a complaint to the regulators in England, Wales, Scotland and Northern Ireland go to

Care Quality Commission www.cqc.org.uk

Care Council for Wales www.cssiw.org.uk

The Scottish Commission for the Regulation of Care www.carecommission.com

The Regulation and Quality Improvement Authority www.rqia.org.uk

Glossary

Accident an undesired or unintended event which results in physical or psychological harm to an individual, damage to property or goods or the environment.

Abuse a violation of a person's human and civil rights by any other person or persons, which usually involves a misuse of power.

Adverse event unanticipated problem involving risk to a person that resulted in harm to them or others. This could include an injury requiring medical treatment.

Breach if your human rights are breached, it means they are ignored.

Challenging behaviour behaviour which puts the safety of the person or others at risk or has a significant impact on the person's or other people's quality of life.

Complaint any expression of unhappiness, whether spoken or written, from or on behalf of a person about a service's provision of, or failure to provide, care and support.

Duty of care those in a professional or other paid capacity, with responsibility for providing support to others, must take reasonable care to avoid acts or omissions that are likely to cause harm to the person or persons they care for or to other people.

Empower to enable an individual to think, behave, take action, and control work and decision making independently.

Error an action that doesn't go as planned, or when a wrong judgement or decision is made that leads to physical or psychological harm.

Ethics a set of beliefs concerning what is wrong and right in human conduct which guide decision making and behaviour.

Incident any event that could have led or did lead to unintended or unexpected harm, loss or damage, e.g. theft, fire, violence, abuse, ill health or infection.

Informed decision a decision where a choice is made by an individual, using relevant information about the advantages and disadvantages of all the possible courses of action.

Mental capacity a person's ability to make their own decisions and to understand the consequences of those decisions.

Near miss when something that could go wrong is identified and prevented and so did not result in injury, illness, or damage – but it had the potential to do so.

Neglect systematically and consistently failing to respond to a person's needs or failing to take actions in their best interests. It can be deliberate, but is not always done on purpose.

Negligence failure to use reasonable care that would be expected of any other person in a similar situation.

Policy a statement or plan of action that clearly sets out an organisation's position or approach on a particular issue.

Power the ability of a person or group of people to exercise authority over another, thereby controlling and influencing others.

Procedure a set of instructions that sets out in detail how a policy should be put into practice and what staff should do in response to a specific situation.

Rights a framework of laws that protects people from harm, sets out what people can say and do and guarantees the right to a fair trial and other basic entitlements, such as the right to respect, equality, etc.

Risk probability or threat of damage, injury, liability, loss, or other negative occurrence which may be prevented through planned action.

Risk assessment a careful examination of what could cause harm to people, so that you can weigh up whether you have taken enough precautions or should do more to prevent harm.

Vulnerable adult a person who is or may be in need of community care services by reason of mental or other disability, age or illness and who is or may be unable to take care of themselves against significant harm or exploitation.

Index

Added to a page number 'g' denotes glossary.